Chef Yan's

Entertaining At Home

Simple, Healthy and Elegant

To Bob

good food
good wine
good fortune

Yan Can Cook

Email: yccook@aol.com   Website: http://www.yancancook.com

Chef Yan's Entertaining at Home

AUTHOR **Martin Yan**

PROJECT COORDINATOR FOR YAN CAN COOK **Stephanie Liu Jan**

FOOD PHOTOGRAPHY **Rosa To**

FOOD STYLIST **Stephanie Liu Jan**

PROP STYLIST **Stephanie Liu Jan** / **Rosa To**

FOOD PHOTOGRAPHY COORDINATOR **Stephanie Liu Jan**

PHOTOGRAPHY CHEFS **Mr. Frank Liou**

Helen Soehalim / **Vivienne Marsh** / **Anthony Tse** / **Julia Lee** /

Luke Fong

TRAVEL PHOTOGRAPHY **Stephanie Liu Jan**

EDITOR **Shek Kin**

DESIGNER **Lee Lai Ying** / **Wong Miu Ling**

First published in Hong Kong in 2000 by Wan Li Book Co., Ltd.

Unit 1, G/F, 5B-5F Ma Hang Chung Rd., Tokwawan, Kowloon, H.K.

TEL **2564 7511**   FAX **2565 5539**

WEBSITE **http://www.wanlibk.com**

ISBN 962-14-1796-1

Yan Can Cook, Inc.

P.O. Box 4755, Foster City, CA 94404, USA

Email: yccook@aol.com

Website: http://www.yancancook.com

Introduction

"If Yan can cook, so can you!" I've been saying that for years, and the message hasn't changed. It really is that simple.

Life on the road is not as glamorous as it sounds. Everybody pitches in to carry equipment and supplies. In the end, a good show makes all our hard work worthwhile. There is nothing like the strong support and positive feedback from our audience.

My philosophy of cooking and eating is pretty simple, too. You can sum it up in six words: Good food, good health, and good living. Over the years, I've consistently advocated eating healthfully without compromising flavor, convenience, or the joy of preparing and sharing food with others. This belief lies at the heart of the "Yan Can Cook" show, my books, and my other projects.

One of my long-term projects involves expanding global awareness and appreciation for Chinese and Asian food. I want to share our culinary treasures with the rest of the world, and I believe that the most effective way to do so is by bringing those cuisines and cultures to a hungry public in a lively, entertaining way. So, how am I doing so far?

Judging from the popularity of Asia's fabulous foods, and from your positive feedback — many thanks! — I'm not doing too shabby a job. And nothing makes me want to invite everyone to the Asian table more than your enthusiasm and support. So, I've collected recipes from many of my shows and classes to create this book for you. All of the dishes are easy to prepare, healthful, colorful, and, of course, delicious. They're great for comfy family meals at home as well as for those occasions when you really want to impress the guests.

The key to an exciting world of appetizing Chinese and Asian dishes is only a few easy recipe steps away. Fire up that wok and I'm sure you'll agree with what I've been telling you all along: You really can cook, too!

Martin Yan

CONTENTS

Tofu & Vegetables

Soups & Starches

Desserts

Glossary of Ingredients

Lobster in Golden Cups

◆ **Ingredients**

2 dried black mushrooms

4 asparagus spears

½ red bell pepper

½ pound shelled lobster or raw shrimp meat

◆ **Marinade**

1 teaspoon rice wine or dry sherry

½ teaspoon cornstarch

¼ teaspoon salt

¼ teaspoon white pepper

◆ **Sauce**

1 tablespoon oyster-flavored sauce

2 teaspoons rice wine or dry sherry

1 ½ teaspoons soy sauce

½ teaspoon sugar

6 egg roll wrappers, trimmed into 5-inch circles

2 tablespoons cooking oil

¼ cup coarsely chopped water chestnuts

½ teaspoon cornstarch dissolved in 1 teaspoon water

◆ **Method**

1. Soak mushrooms in warm water to cover until softened, about 15 minutes; drain. Trim and discard stems. Coarsely chop caps. Snap off and discard tough ends of asparagus; coarsely chop spears. Remove and discard seeds from bell pepper; coarsely chop.

2. Cut lobster meat into ½ inch pieces. Combine marinade ingredients in a bowl. Add lobster; stir to coat. Let stand for 10 minutes. Combine sauce ingredients in a bowl.

3. Preheat oven to 325°F. Lightly coat muffin tin with cooking spray. Place a wrapper in each of six cups in tin. Using a ¼ cup measure, press down on wrapper to form a hollow cup. Bake until wrappers turn crispy and golden brown, 6 to 8 minutes. Remove baked wrappers from tin and let cool.

4. Place a wok over high heat until hot. Add oil, swirling to coat sides. Add lobster and stir-fry for 1 minute. Remove and set aside. Add asparagus, bell pepper, water chestnuts, mushrooms, and sauce; stir-fry for 1 minute. Return lobster and add cornstarch solution; cook, stirring, until sauce thickens. Spoon lobster mixture equally among baked cups.

Makes 6 pastry cups

Duck Crystal Wrap

◆Ingredients

4 dried black mushrooms

◆Sauce

⅓ cup chicken broth
2 tablespoons oyster-flavored sauce
2 teaspoons rice wine or dry sherry
½ teaspoon cornstarch

2 tablespoons cooking oil
½ shallot, minced
1 cup diced barbecued duck
1 teaspoon chopped pickled ginger
¼ cup diced pineapple
¼ cup chopped water chestnuts
1 tablespoon chopped cilantro

1 green onion, thinly sliced
Hoisin sauce
12 small iceberg lettuce cups or Belgian endive leaves

◆Method

1. Soak mushrooms in warm water to cover until softened, about 15 minutes; drain. Trim and discard stems. Coarsely chop caps.

2. Combine sauce ingredients in a bowl; set aside.

3. Place a wok over high heat until hot. Add oil, swirling to coat sides. Add shallot; cook, stirring, until fragrant, about 10 seconds. Add duck; stir-fry for 1 minute. Add mushrooms, ginger, pineapple, water chestnuts, cilantro, and green onion; stir-fry for 1 minute. Add sauce; cook, stirring, until sauce boils and thickens.

4. To eat, spread a small amount of hoisin sauce on a lettuce cup, spoon in some duck mixture, wrap up in lettuce cup, and eat out of hand.

Here I am in one of Beijing's most famous Peking duck restaurants, slaving in front of a hot oven as I learn how to make the restaurant's crispy-skinned delicacy.

Makes 4 to 6 servings

TIPS

Old ginger, which is fibrous, is used to season soups and other dishes where a spicy ginger flavor is desired. Younger ginger is sliced, shredded, or minced to use in stir-fry dishes. It can also be pickled.

Lobster-Fruit Salad

◆ Ingredients

½ pound shelled raw lobster meat

◆ Marinade

1 teaspoon rice wine or dry sherry
½ teaspoon sesame oil
½ teaspoon salt
¼ teaspoon white pepper

◆ Dressing

½ cup mayonnaise
2 to 3 tablespoons lemon juice
2 tablespoons condensed milk

½ cup each cantaloupe, honeydew, and watermelon balls
½ cup diced mango
½ cup canned longans, drained
¼ cup red seedless grapes

◆ Method

1. Combine marinade ingredients in a bowl. Add lobster; stir to coat. Let stand for 10 minutes.

2. Combine dressing ingredients in a bowl; set aside.

3. Poach lobster in a pot of boiling water for 2 minutes; drain. Let cool; cut into ½ inch pieces.

4. Place lobster and fruits in a large salad bowl. Add dressing and toss to coat.

Note: You can substitute raw shrimp for the lobster, if desired.

Makes 4 to 6 servings

It's a good idea to be picky when choosing tea, but you don't have to go as far as I do. I went all the way to the West Lake region of China to pick some of the best dragon well tea leaves.

Crispy Crab Claws

◆ Ingredients

8 crab claws

½ pound raw shrimp

◆ Marinade

½ egg white, lightly beaten

1 green onion, white part only, finely chopped

1 teaspoon rice wine or dry sherry

¼ teaspoon salt

⅛ teaspoon white pepper

◆ Sauce

¼ cup chicken broth

2 tablespoons ketchup

2 teaspoons rice vinegar

1 teaspoon chili garlic sauce

1 teaspoon soy sauce

1¼ teaspoons sugar

½ teaspoon cornstarch

Cooking oil for deep-frying

½ cup all-purpose flour

2 eggs, lightly beaten

1 cup panko (Japanese bread crumbs)

◆ Method

1. Shell crab claws, leaving pinchers intact. Shell and devein shrimp; finely chop. Combine marinade ingredients in a bowl. Add shrimp and stir to coat. Let stand for 10 minutes. Combine sauce ingredients in a small saucepan; set aside.

2. Using a spoon, mold 1 heaping tablespoon shrimp mixture around each crab claw. Smooth surface with wet hands. Repeat with remaining crab claws and shrimp mixture.

3. Heat oil in a wok to 350°F. Dust crab claws with flour. Shake to remove excess. Dip into egg; drain briefly, then coat with panko. Deep-fry crab claws until golden brown, about 3 minutes. Remove and drain on paper towels.

4. Heat sauce over medium heat and cook, stirring, until sauce boils and thickens. Serve sauce alongside crab claws.

Makes 8 stuffed crab claws

TIPS

To deep-fry seafood: Heat cooking oil to 350°F; reduce heat to medium to medium-low. Add seafood and deep-fry until golden brown. Seafood will be more evenly cooked when using this method.

Golden Fish with Sweet Corn

◆ Ingredients

¾ pound firm white fish fillets, such as sea bass or red snapper, about ¼-inch thick

◆ Marinade

1 tablespoon rice wine or dry sherry
2 teaspoons soy sauce
1 teaspoon minced ginger
1 teaspoon cornstarch

◆ Sauce

¾ cup chicken broth
½ cup cream-style corn
½ teaspoon sesame oil
½ teaspoon sugar
¼ teaspoon salt

2 eggs, lightly beaten
½ cup dried bread crumbs
4 tablespoons cooking oil
1 jalapeño or serrano chile, seeded and coarsely chopped
3 tablespoons crabmeat
1 cup cooked corn

◆ Method

1. Combine marinade ingredients in a bowl. Add fish and turn to coat. Let stand for 10 minutes. Combine sauce ingredients in a bowl; set aside.

2. Heat 3 tablespoons oil in a wide non-stick frying pan over high heat. Dip fish in egg, drain briefly, then coat with bread crumbs. Cook fish in hot oil, turning once, until golden brown, 3 to 4 minutes. Remove and drain on paper towels; keep warm.

3. Heat remaining 1 tablespoon oil in a wok over high heat. Add chile; cook, stirring, until fragrant, about 10 seconds. Add crabmeat and corn; stir-fry for 30 seconds. Add sauce; bring to a boil and cook, stirring, until slightly thickened.

4. To serve, arrange fish on a serving plate and pour sauce over top.

Makes 4 to 6 servings

TIPS

Corn is native to the American continents and was exported to Europe and Asia. In northern China, corn is dried, ground into cornmeal, and used in many dishes. It is rich in vitamins B_1, B_2, and B_6, and starch. It is believed that corn can regulate cholesterol absorption and lower blood pressure.

Fish in Eight Treasure Sauce

◆ Ingredients

4 dried black mushrooms

3 tablespoons dried shrimp

½ teaspoon salt

¼ teaspoon white pepper

1 whole fish (1½ to 2 pounds), such as sea bass or red snapper, cleaned and scaled

◆ Sauce

1 cup chicken broth

1 tablespoon oyster-flavored sauce

2 teaspoons chili garlic sauce

2 teaspoons rice wine or dry sherry

2 teaspoons sesame oil

2 teaspoons sugar

¼ teaspoon ground toasted Sichuan peppercorns

3 tablespoons cooking oil

2 teaspoons minced garlic

1 green onion, thinly sliced

2 jalapeño or serrano chiles, seeded and coarsely chopped

¼ cup chopped water chestnuts

¼ pound pressed bean curd, coarsely chopped

2 tablespoons chopped Sichuan preserved vegetable

1 teaspoon cornstarch dissolved in 2 teaspoons water

◆ Method

1. Soak mushrooms and shrimp in separate bowls in warm water to cover until softened, about 15 minutes; drain. Trim and discard mushrooms stems. Coarsely chop caps. Coarsely chop shrimp.

2. Sprinkle salt and pepper over both sides of fish. Set aside for 10 minutes. Combine sauce ingredients in a bowl; set aside.

3. Place a wok over high heat until hot. Add 2 tablespoons oil, swirling to coat sides. Add fish; pan-fry until golden brown, 3 to 4 minutes on each side. Remove from wok and keep warm.

4. Heat remaining 1 tablespoon in wok over high heat. Add garlic, green onion, chiles, and shrimp; cook, stirring, until fragrant, about 10 seconds. Add mushrooms, water chestnuts, bean curd, and preserved vegetable; stir-fry for 1 minute.

5. Add sauce and bring to a boil. Add cornstarch solution and cook, stirring, until sauce boils and thickens.

6. To serve, arrange fish on a serving plate and pour sauce over top.

Makes 4 to 6 servings

Steamed Fish with Quail Eggs

◆ Ingredients

1 firm white fish fillet (about ¾ pound) with skin intact, such as sea bass or red snapper, about 1 inch thick

◆ Marinade

½ teaspoon cornstarch
¼ teaspoon salt
¼ teaspoon white pepper

◆ Sauce

¼ cup chicken broth
1 teaspoon oyster-flavored sauce
⅛ teaspoon sugar

2 tablespoons julienned Sichuan preserved vegetable
3 hard-boiled eggs, shelled and cut in half or 6 hard-boiled quail eggs, shelled
1 green onion, cut into 1 inch pieces
1 teaspoon cornstarch dissolved in 2 teaspoons water

◆ Method

1. Cut fish fillet into six 3 inch x 2½ inch x 1½ inch pieces. Score skin side of each fillet to make a v-shaped pocket.

2. Combine marinade ingredients in a bowl. Add fish fillets and turn to coat. Let stand for 10 minutes. Combine sauce ingredients in a small saucepan; set aside.

3. Place about 1 heaping teaspoon preserved vegetable, one egg half (or one whole quail egg), and one piece of green onion into each fillet pocket. Place fish in a heat-proof glass pie dish.

4. Prepare a wok for steaming. Cover and steam fish over high heat until fish turns opaque, about 6 minutes. Remove and drain liquid from fish. Place fish on a serving plate and keep warm.

5. Bring sauce to a boil over medium-high heat. Add cornstarch solution and cook, stirring, until sauce thickens. Pour sauce over top of fish.

The best way to appreciate the Imperial Banquet is to dress for the occasion.

TIPS

Steaming fish: Place fish on a heat-proof dish lined with long pieces of green onions. Place dish in steamer when water is at a rolling boil. The green onions keep fish from sticking to the dish. They also create a space between the fish and the plate, allowing steam to circulate under the fish which results in more uniform cooking.

Makes 4 to 6 servings

Prawns in Wine Sauce

◆Ingredients

1 pound jumbo raw prawns

◆Marinade

1 egg white, lightly beaten

2 teaspoons rice wine or dry sherry

2 teaspoons cornstarch

1/4 teaspoon salt

1/4 teaspoon white pepper

◆Sauce

2/3 cup chicken broth

2 tablespoons rice wine or dry sherry

1/4 teaspoon sugar

1/4 teaspoon salt

1/8 teaspoon white pepper

1 tablespoon cooking oil

1 1/2 tablespoons cornstarch dissolved in 1/2 cup milk

2 teaspoons toasted sesame seeds

Shredded basil for garnish

◆Method

1. Shell and devein prawns, leaving tails intact; butterfly them and rinse out sand veins. Combine marinade ingredients in a bowl. Add prawns and stir to coat. Let stand for 10 minutes.

2. Combine sauce ingredients in a small bowl; set aside.

3. Place a wok over high heat until hot. Add oil, swirling to coat sides. Add prawns and cook until they turn pink, 2 to 3 minutes. Remove prawns from wok.

4. Heat sauce in a wok over medium heat and cook until sauce boils. Add cornstarch solution and cook, stirring, until sauce boils and thickens. Return prawns to wok and toss to coat. Sprinkle with sesame seeds and basil.

Makes 4 servings

Pei Pa Jumbo Prawns

◆**Ingredients**

8 jumbo raw prawns
½ pound raw shrimp

◆**Marinade**

½ egg white, lightly beaten
2 teaspoons rice wine or dry sherry
½ teaspoon sesame oil
1 tablespoon cornstarch
½ teaspoon salt
¼ teaspoon sugar
¼ teaspoon white pepper

1 tablespoon minced water chestnuts
Cornstarch for dusting
1 sheet Japanese seaweed (nori), cut into thin strips

¼ cup julienned cooked ham
3 tablespoons cooking oil
Prepared sweet and sour sauce

◆**Method**

1. Shell and devein prawns and shrimp, leaving tails intact on prawns. Butterfly prawns and rinse out sand veins. Combine marinade ingredients in a bowl. Add prawns and shrimp and stir to coat. Remove shrimp and finely mince. Mix water chestnuts with shrimp.

2. Flatten each butterflied prawn, then dust, cut side down, with cornstarch. Shake to remove excess. Spread about 1 tablespoon shrimp mixture over each prawn; smooth the mounded filling with a wet knife. Center a strip of seaweed on filling; place a strip of ham on each side of seaweed. Fill remaining prawns with shrimp mixture.

3. Place a wok over medium heat until hot. Add oil, swirling to coat sides. Add prawns, filling side down, and cook until prawns turn pink, about 2 minutes. Serve with sweet and sour sauce.

Makes 4 servings

Pei Pa Prawns would always remind me of the fabulous Imperial Banquet and the wonderful experience of riding the sedan chair as "Emperor For A Day".

Sweet and Sour Pinecone Fish

◆ Ingredients

1 firm white fish fillet (about ¾ pound) with skin intact, such as sea bass or red snapper, about 1-inch thick

◆ Marinade

½ teaspoon sesame oil
½ teaspoon salt
¼ teaspoon white pepper

◆ Sauce

½ cup chicken broth
⅓ cup rice vinegar
2 tablespoons chili garlic sauce
¼ cup sugar
½ teaspoon salt

2 eggs, lightly beaten
½ cup all-purpose flour
Cooking oil for deep-frying
½ small onion, diced

1 teaspoon minced ginger
1 jalapeño or serrano chile, seeded and finely chopped
¼ cup diced pineapple
2 teaspoons cornstarch dissolved in 4 teaspoons water
½ cup toasted pine nuts

◆ Method

1. Score skinless side of fish with shallow diagonal cuts; score again at a 90 degree angle to the first cuts. Cut fillet into 3 inch squares. Combine marinade ingredients in a bowl and add fish; turn to coat. Let stand for 10 minutes.

2. Combine sauce ingredients in a bowl; set aside.

3. Dip fish squares in egg, drain briefly, then coat with flour. Shake to remove excess. Heat oil in a wok to 375°F. Deep-fry fish, turning once, until golden brown, 2 to 3 minutes. Remove and drain on paper towels. Keep warm.

4. Place a wok over medium-high heat until hot. Add 1 tablespoon oil, swirling to coat sides. Add onion, ginger, and chile; cook, stirring, until fragrant, about 10 seconds. Add pineapple and sauce; cook for 30 seconds. Add cornstarch solution and cook, stirring, until sauce boils and thickens.

5. To serve, arrange fish on a serving plate. Pour sauce over fish and sprinkle with pine nuts.

Makes 4 to 6 servings

TIPS

Heat cooking oil to near smoking, then turn off heat before adding fish to be deep-fried. Turn heat back on and continue cooking. Fish deep-fried by this method will not fall apart. Use only as much oil as needed, and add fish carefully to prevent oil from splashing.

Clay Pot Garlic Fish

◆ Ingredients

1 pound firm white fish fillets, such as sea bass or red snapper, about ¾ inch thick

◆ Marinade

2 tablespoons rice wine or dry sherry
1 tablespoon soy sauce
2 teaspoons sesame oil
1 teaspoon minced ginger
¼ teaspoon white pepper

◆ Sauce

⅓ cup chicken broth
2 teaspoons miso (fermented soybean paste)
2 teaspoons dark soy sauce
2 teaspoons sesame oil
1 teaspoon sugar

3 tablespoons cooking oil
16 cloves garlic, deep-fried
2 tablespoons rice wine or dry sherry
4 green onions, cut into 2 inch pieces
½ teaspoon cornstarch dissolved in 1 teaspoon water

◆ Method

1. Cut fish into 2 inch x 1 inch pieces. Combine marinade ingredients in a bowl. Add fish and turn to coat. Let stand for 10 minutes.

2. Combine sauce ingredients in a bowl; set aside.

3. Place a wok over high heat until hot. Add 2 tablespoons oil, swirling to coat sides. Add fish fillets and pan-fry until golden brown, 1 to 2 minutes on each side. Remove fish from wok.

4. Add remaining 1 tablespoon oil to clay pot over medium heat until hot. Add garlic; cook, stirring, until fragrant, about 10 seconds. Add fish and wine; cook for 1 minute. Add green onions and sauce. Bring to a boil; reduce heat, cover, and simmer for 5 minutes. Add cornstarch solution and cook, stirring, until sauce thickens.

Makes 4 to 6 servings

TIPS

Deep-fry garlic cloves before adding to a stewed or braised dish. This mellows the garlic's sharpness, resulting in a nice sweet flavor. Deep-fried garlic cloves are a little drier and will absorb the flavors of the cooking juices.

Five-flavored Smoked Fish

◆ Ingredients

1 pound salmon fillet, 1 inch thick

Flour for dusting

◆ Marinade

1 tablespoon soy sauce

½ teaspoon salt

¼ teaspoon Chinese five-spice

¼ teaspoon sugar

◆ Smoking Mixture

⅔ cup uncooked rice

1 tablespoon black tea leaves

2 teaspoons Chinese five-spice

2 teaspoons packed brown sugar

3 whole star anise

2 tablespoons cooking oil

◆ Method

1. Cut fish into 3 inch squares. Combine marinade ingredients in a bowl. Add fish and turn to coat. Cover and refrigerate for 2 hours.

2. Dust fish with flour. Shake to remove excess.

3. Combine smoking mixture ingredients in a bowl.

4. Place a wok over high heat until hot. Add cooking oil, swirling to coat sides. Add fish and pan-fry until golden brown, about 2 minutes on each side. Remove and drain on paper towels.

5. Spread smoking mixture evenly in a foil-lined wok. Set a round cake rack over smoking mixture. Place fish on rack and place wok over high heat until it begins to smoke. Cover wok with a foil-lined lid; reduce heat to medium-low and smoke until fish flakes with a fork, about 7 minutes.

6. Turn off heat and allow to sit, covered, for 5 minutes. Serve fish hot or cold.

Makes 4 to 6 servings

Crab with Wine Sauce

◆ Ingredients

1 live Dungeness crab or 4 blue shell crabs

4 egg whites, lightly beaten

⅓ cup chicken broth

2 tablespoons rice wine or dry sherry

◆ Sauce

2 tablespoons rice wine or dry sherry

1 teaspoon minced ginger

1 teaspoon sesame oil

¼ teaspoon salt

◆ Method

1. Parboil crab in a pot of boiling water for 2 minutes. Drain, rinse with cold water, and drain again. Clean crab. Twist off claws and legs. Cut body into 4 pieces. (For blue shell crabs, cut body into two pieces.) Reserve shell.

2. Combine sauce ingredients in a bowl; set aside.

3. Combine egg whites, chicken broth, and wine; pour into a heat-proof serving dish. Arrange crab pieces over egg white mixture; cover with crab shell.

4. Prepare a wok for steaming. Cover and steam crab over high heat until crab turns red and egg whites turn opaque, 10 to 12 minutes. Remove shell and pour sauce over crab pieces. Return shell and steam 2 more minutes.

Wine has always inspired art and poetry-especially in the kitchen. As I stand among the jars of Shao Hsing wine, my mind wanders to the masterpieces I'll make it at home.

TIPS

Rub your hands with strong tea, lemon slices, rice wine, chrysanthemum leaves, pea shoots, or toothpaste to rid them of the fishy smell after shelling crab.

Makes 4 servings

◆ Ingredients

1 piece dried tangerine peel
12 small raw shrimp
¼ teaspoon salt
Dash of white pepper
½ pound white fish fillet
6 tofu puffs
1 tablespoon finely chopped bacon
1 green onion, finely chopped

◆ Marinade

1 teaspoon sesame oil
½ teaspoon salt
¼ teaspoon white pepper

◆ Sauce

½ cup chicken broth
1½ teaspoons oyster-flavored sauce
1 teaspoon rice wine or dry sherry
1 teaspoon sesame oil
½ teaspoon sugar

1 tablespoon cooking oil
1 teaspoon cornstarch dissolved in
2 teaspoons water

◆ Method

1. Soak tangerine peel in warm water to cover until softened, about 15 minutes; drain. Finely chop and set aside.

2. Shell and devein shrimp, leaving tails intact; butterfly them and rinse out sand veins. Combine shrimp, salt, and pepper in a bowl; stir to coat. Let stand for 10 minutes. Finely chop or grind fish fillet into a coarse paste.

3. Cut tofu puffs in half and hollow them out. Set tofu puff halves aside and finely chop unused tofu pieces.

4. Combine marinade ingredients in a bowl. Add fish paste, bacon, green onion, tangerine peel, and chopped tofu; stir to mix well. Let stand for 10 minutes.

5. Combine sauce ingredients in a bowl; set aside.

6. Spoon fish paste mixture equally among tofu puff halves. Place a shrimp on top of each.

7. Place a wok over high heat until hot. Add oil, swirling to coat sides. Add tofu puffs, shrimp-side down, and pan-fry for 30 seconds. Reduce heat to low. Turn puffs over; add sauce, cover and simmer for 5 to 6 minutes. Add cornstarch solution and cook, stirring, until sauce boils and thickens.

Makes 4 to 6 servings

TIPS

Hollow out tofu puffs before stuffing. Reserve the unused tofu pieces to add to the filling.

Scallops and Crispy Puffs

◆ Batter

1 cup water
½ teaspoon cooking oil
¾ cup all-purpose flour
¼ cup cornstarch
¾ teaspoon baking powder
¼ teaspoon sugar

◆ Milk Pudding

⅓ cup unsweetened coconut milk
⅓ cup evaporated milk
⅓ cup chicken broth
¼ cup water
⅔ cup cornstarch
⅓ cup sugar
¼ teaspoon salt

¾ pound sea scallops
2 teaspoons cornstarch
Cooking oil for deep-frying
Cornstarch for dusting
1 teaspoon minced ginger
½ carrot, thinly sliced
1 green onion, cut into 1½ inch pieces
¼ cup chicken broth
½ teaspoon salt
½ teaspoon cornstarch dissolved in 1 teaspoon water

◆ Method

1. Combine batter ingredients in a bowl; whisk until smooth. Refrigerate batter for at least 30 minutes.

2. Combine milk pudding ingredients in a bowl; whisk until smooth. Pour pudding mixture into an oiled heat-proof glass pie dish.

3. Prepare a wok for steaming. Cover and steam pudding over high heat until firm, 10 to 12 minutes. Remove and let cool; refrigerate until chilled. Cut pudding into 2 inch x 1 inch pieces; set aside.

4. Heat cooking oil for deep-frying over high heat. Dust pudding pieces with cornstarch; shake to remove excess. Dip them in the batter, then drop in the hot oil, deep-fry for 1 to 2 minutes or until golden brown. Remove and drain on paper towels. Keep warm.

5. Combine scallops and 2 teaspoons cornstarch in a bowl; stir to coat. Let stand for 10 minutes.

6. Place a wok over high heat until hot. Add 2 tablespoons cooking oil, swirling to coat sides. Add ginger; cook, stirring until fragrant, about 10 seconds. Add scallops; stir-fry until scallops turn opaque, about 1 minute. Remove scallops from wok. Add carrot, green onion, chicken broth, and salt; cover and cook until carrot is crisp-tender, 1 to 2 minutes. Return scallops. Add cornstarch solution and cook, stirring, until sauce boils and thickens.

7. To serve, place scallop mixture in center of a serving plate. Arrange crispy pudding pieces around scallops.

Makes 4 to 6 servings

34

Quenelles with Shrimp

◆ Ingredients

8 to 10 small raw shrimp
⅛ teaspoon salt

◆ Sauce

½ cup chicken broth
½ cup milk
½ teaspoon sugar
½ teaspoon salt

◆ Egg White Puffs

2 to 3 egg whites
⅛ teaspoon salt
1 tablespoon all-purpose flour
1½ teaspoons cornstarch

5 cups water
2 tablespoons vinegar
1 cup chicken broth
2 tablespoons cornstarch dissolved
   in ¼ cup water
8 to 10 cilantro leaves
1 tablespoon fish roe, optional

◆ Method

1. Combine shrimp and salt in a bowl; stir to coat. Let stand for 10 minutes. Combine sauce ingredients in a small saucepan; set aside.

2. Combine egg whites and salt; beat until light and foamy. Add flour and cornstarch; continue to beat until soft peaks form. Fill 8 to 10 oiled Chinese ceramic soup spoons equally with egg white mixture, smoothing tops with a wet butter knife.

3. Bring water and vinegar to a boil in a large pot. Reduce heat to low and place filled soup spoons gently in water; egg white puffs will slip off spoon. Poach for 2 to 3 minutes, turning once. Lift out and remove egg white puffs; drain and set aside.

4. Bring chicken broth to a boil in a pot. Reduce heat to low and add shrimp. Poach shrimp for 1 to 2 minutes. Remove and drain.

5. Bring sauce to a boil over medium-high heat. Add cornstarch solution and cook, stirring until sauce thickens. To serve, pour sauce on a serving plate and arrange egg white puffs on top. Place shrimp on each puff; garnish with a cilantro leaf and a small amount of fish roe.

TIPS

Add a teaspoon of vinegar to simmering liquid when poaching eggs. The acid in the vinegar helps the proteins in the egg white cook more quickly.

Makes 8 to 10 puffs

Poached Seafood Bundles

◆ Ingredients

12 medium raw shrimp

◆ Marinade

¼ teaspoon salt

⅛ teaspoon white pepper

◆ Sauce

⅓ cup chicken broth

1 tablespoon soy sauce

1 tablespoon balsamic vinegar

2 teaspoons sesame oil

2 teaspoons hoisin sauce

1 tablespoon packed brown sugar

2 pieces dried gourd strips or 12 garlic chives

1 sheet dried Chinese-style seaweed

12 sugar snap peas

¼ cup matchstick pieces jicama

¼ cup matchstick pieces cooked ham

2 cups chicken broth

1 teaspoon cornstach dissolved in 2 teaspoons water

◆ Method

1. Shell and devein shrimp, leaving tails intact. Butterfly shrimp and rinse out sand veins. Combine marinade ingredients in a small bowl. Add shrimp and stir to coat. Let stand for 10 minutes. Combine sauce ingredients in a saucepan; set aside.

2. Soak gourd strips in warm water to cover until softened, about 15 minutes; cut into 5 inch strips. If using chives, blanch them in boiling water for 1 minute; cut into 5 inch strips. Soak seaweed briefly in warm water to soften; cut into twelve 4 inch x 1 inch strips.

3. Blanch snap peas in boiling water until crisp-tender, about 2 minutes; drain.

4. To make each bundle: Put together in a pile one piece each of shrimp, jicama, ham, and snap pea. Wrap a strip of seaweed around bundle; secure and tie with a gourd strip. Prepare remaining bundles.

5. Bring chicken broth to a boil in a saucepan over high heat. Reduce heat so that broth is just bubbling. Add seaweed bundles and poach until shrimp turn pink, 1 to 2 minutes. Remove shrimp bundles, drain, and arrange on a serving plate; keep warm.

6. Place sauce over high heat and bring to a boil. Add cornstarch solution and cook, stirring, until sauce thickens. Pour sauce over shrimp bundles and serve.

TIPS

Whether they wind up flavoring chips or mingling with sour cream atop a baked potato, chives have become so standard in American kitchens that it's almost easy not to notice them. I bet that'll never happen with garlic chives, also known as Chinese chives or yellow chives. These flavorful herbs have a delicate onion-garlic flavor that promises never to become "background noise" in the profile of a dish. Add them to stir-fries and noodle dishes. Or, chop and mix them with shrimp and seafood for pungent fillings for steamed dim sum dumplings. They're practical, too: when blanched to soften, they become attractive "ties" for bundling shreds of vegetables and seafood or cinching the top of dumpling wrappers to form little sacks. Look for green, wide, grass-like chives or shorter yellow chives. If you're lucky, you may even find flowering chives with firm stalks and edible blossoms at the tips.

Makes 12 bundles

Lemongrass Spiced Prawns

◆ Ingredients

8 jumbo raw prawns

◆ Marinade

¼ teaspoon salt

¼ teaspoon white pepper

◆ Sauce

2 tablespoons ketchup

1 tablespoon satay sauce

1 tablespoon XO sauce, optional

2 teaspoons dark soy sauce

2 teaspoons seasoned rice vinegar

2 teaspoons rice wine or dry sherry

1 teaspoon sesame oil

1 teaspoon sugar

2 tablespoons cooking oil

2 teaspoons minced garlic

1 stalk lemongrass (bottom 6 inches only), thinly sliced

1 jalapeño or serrano chile, seeded and minced

¼ cup finely chopped carrot

1 tablespoon butter

◆ Method

1. Shell and devein prawns. Butterfly prawns and rinse out sand veins. Combine marinade ingredients in a bowl. Add prawns and turn to coat. Let stand for 10 minutes. Combine sauce ingredients in a bowl; set aside.

2. Place a wok over high heat until hot. Add oil, swirling to coat sides. Add garlic, lemongrass, and chile; cook, stirring, for 30 seconds. Add carrot; stir-fry for 30 seconds. Add sauce and cook for 1 minute. Remove and let cool.

3. Flatten a butterflied prawn on a clean work surface. Spread one heaping tablespoon lemongrass mixture over prawn. Repeat with remaining prawns and lemongrass mixture.

4. Melt butter in a frying pan over low heat. Add prawns, stuffed side down; cover and simmer for 5 minutes.

Makes 4 to 6 servings

TIPS

If you've ever had the pleasure of dining at a traditional, upscale Hong Kong-style seafood restaurant patronized by gourmands of Chinese cuisine, you may have enjoyed a pungent condiment made from dried shrimp and scallops, red chile peppers, shrimp roe, shallots, garlic, and spices. Can you remember its name? It's not tough to recall: It's called XO sauce, and it's truly eXtraOrdinary. (How's that for a clue as to what its name means?) Developed by Hong Kong's gourmet chefs, it also goes by a more luxurious, but equally appropriate, nickname, "The Caviar of the Orient." Add a hint to sauces for noodles or short ribs and you'll be surprised at what flavors it awakens. I like to use it as a condiment with almost anything, or even as an appetizer by itself. It has caviar beaten by a long-shot.

Beggar's Chicken

◆ Marinade

2 teaspoons minced ginger
1 green onion, thinly sliced
½ cup hoisin sauce
2 teaspoons dark soy sauce
1½ teaspoons soy sauce
1 teaspoon sugar
½ teaspoon Chinese five-spice

1 whole chicken fryer (about 3 lbs), cleaned
2 dried lotus leaves

◆ Baker's Clay

9 egg whites
8 cups salt

◆ Stuffing

2 tablespoons cooking oil
1 tablespoon shredded ginger
½ small onion, thinly sliced
¼ pound pork, shredded
¼ cup julienned Sichuan preserved vegetable
2 tablespoons rice wine or dry sherry
1 whole star anise

Foil to enclose chicken

◆ Method

1. Combine marinade ingredients in a large bowl. Reserve 2 tablespoons marinade; set aside. Add chicken; turn to coat on all sides and rub inside and out. Cover and refrigerate for 1 hour.

2. Bring a large pot of water to a boil. Add lotus leaves; reduce heat and simmer until softened, about 15 minutes. Drain and set aside. Combine baker's clay ingredients in a bowl; set aside.

3. Place a wok over high heat until hot. Add oil, swirling to coat sides. Add ginger and onion; cook, stirring, until onion is soft, about 1 minute. Add pork; stir-fry for 1 minute. Add preserved vegetable, wine, and star anise; cook for 1 minute. Add reserved marinade; mix well. Let stuffing cool.

4. Place stuffing inside chicken; enclose with skewers. Spread 1 lotus leaf on a clean flat work surface; cover with second leaf. Place chicken in center of leaves; fold leaves over to enclose chicken. Fold foil around chicken to enclose.

5. Preheat oven to 450°F. Cover a baking sheet with foil; spread half of clay mixture in the shape of a circle about 1 inch thick. Place wrapped chicken in center of clay mixture. Spread remaining clay over entire chicken to enclose. Bake, breast side up, for 1¼ hours.

6. Remove from oven; let rest for 15 minutes. With a heavy hammer or cleaver, break open clay shell. Fold back wrappers and serve.

TIPS

For some traditionalists, a dish of Beggar's Chicken just wouldn't be the same if it weren't wrapped in a big, green lotus leaf. Although you can omit the lotus leaf wrapper from this recipe if you can't find one, it makes quite an impressive presentation and lends a smoky, aromatic flavor to the chicken wrapped within. Although different recipes call for different preparations of the lotus leaves, they're normally soaked or boiled to soften them for wrapping; when dried, they're brittle and prone to break. Look for lotus leaves wrapped in plastic packages. If you can find any, keep them in a cool, dry place for several months.

Makes 6 servings

Chicken with Chrysanthemum

◆ Ingredients

¾ pound boneless, skinless chicken

◆ Marinade

2 teaspoons rice wine or dry sherry
1 teaspoon oyster-flavored sauce

◆ Sauce

¼ cup chicken broth
1 tablespoon soy sauce
2 teaspoons rice wine or dry sherry
1 teaspoon sugar
¼ teaspoon salt

1 chrysanthemum flower
3 tablespoons rice wine or dry sherry
2 tablespoons cooking oil
2 teaspoons minced ginger

½ small carrot, thinly sliced
1 green onion, thinly sliced
½ teaspoon cornstarch dissolved in 1 teaspoon water

◆ Method

1. Cut chicken into bite-sized pieces. Combine marinade ingredients in a bowl. Add chicken and stir to coat. Let stand for 10 minutes. Combine sauce ingredients in a bowl; set aside.

2. Remove petals from chrysanthemum flower and soak in rice wine for 10 minutes. Remove from wine and drain; set aside.

3. Place a wok over high heat until hot. Add oil, swirling to coat sides. Add ginger; cook, stirring, until fragrant, about 10 seconds. Add chicken; stir-fry for 1 minute. Add carrot, green onion, and sauce; cover and cook until carrot is crisp tender, 1 to 2 minutes. Add cornstarch solution and cook, stirring, until sauce boils and thickens. Transfer to a serving plate. Sprinkle with chrysanthemum petals.

Makes 4 servings

Braised Chicken and Mushrooms

◆ Ingredients

4 to 6 dried black mushrooms

2 ounces dried cellophane noodles

¼ pound boneless, skinless chicken

◆ Marinade

2 teaspoons soy sauce

½ teaspoon cornstarch

◆ Sauce

1 tablespoon dark soy sauce

1 tablespoon oyster-flavored sauce

½ teaspoon salt

½ teaspoon sugar

10 garlic chives

2 ounces enoki mushrooms

1½ cups chicken broth

2 tablespoons julienned cooked ham

1 piece pressed bean curd, julienned

1½ teaspoons cornstarch dissolved in 2 teaspoons water

◆ Method

1. Soak mushrooms and noodles separately in warm water to cover until softened, about 15 minutes; drain. Trim and discard mushroom stems. Julienne caps. Set noodles aside.

2. Thinly slice chicken. Combine marinade ingredients in a bowl. Add chicken and stir to coat. Let stand for 10 minutes. Combine sauce ingredients in a bowl; set aside.

3. Blanch chives in boiling water for 1 minute; drain. Cut into 4-inch lengths. Divide enoki mushrooms into 6 portions; tie each portion with a piece of chive.

4. Bring broth to a boil in a pot; reduce heat to medium. Add noodles; cook for 4 minutes. Add chicken, ham, bean curd, black mushrooms, and sauce; cook for 2 minutes. Reduce heat to low; add enoki mushrooms; cook for 1 minute.

5. Add cornstarch solution and cook, stirring, until thickened.

TIPS

Yellow chives are Chinese green chives which have been shielded from sunlight when they are growing. Chives contain small amounts of proteins, carbohydrates, and vitamin C.

Makes 4 to 6 servings

Chestnut Chicken

◆Ingredients

½ pound boneless, skinless chicken

◆Marinade

1 tablespoon soy sauce
2 teaspoons rice wine or dry sherry
1 teaspoon cornstarch

2 tablespoons cooking oil
1 tablespoon minced garlic
1 teaspoon minced ginger
½ small onion, diced
1 small red bell pepper, cut into
   ½ inch squares
1 stalk celery, diced

½ cup chicken broth
2 tablespoons soy sauce
1 teaspoon sesame oil
½ teaspoon sugar
1 teaspoon cornstarch dissolved in
   2 teaspoons water
¾ cup peeled roasted chestnuts

◆Method

1. Cut chicken into ½ inch cubes. Combine marinade ingredients in a bowl. Add chicken and stir to coat. Let stand for 10 minutes.

2. Place a wok over high heat until hot. Add cooking oil, swirling to coat sides. Add garlic and ginger; cook, stirring, until fragrant, about 10 seconds. Add chicken; stir-fry until opaque, about 2 minutes. Add onion, bell pepper, celery, and broth; stir-fry for 2 minutes.

3. Add soy sauce, sesame oil, and sugar; mix well. Add cornstarch solution and cook, stirring, until sauce thickens. Stir in chestnuts just before serving.

Makes 4 servings

Chicken and Beef Rolls

◆Marinade

1 tablespoon rice wine or dry sherry
1 tablespoon soy sauce
2 teaspoons cornstarch
¼ teaspoon salt
¼ teaspoon white pepper

½ pound boneless tender beef, sliced paper thin
2 boneless, skinless chicken breast halves
1 apple, peeled and cored
1 kiwifruit, peeled
1 small mango, peeled and seeded
1 pear, peeled and cored
2 tablespoons cooking oil

◆Sauce A

½ cup diced mango, pureed
3 tablespoons chicken broth
1 tablespoon seasoned rice vinegar
1 tablespoon honey
¼ teaspoon salt

◆Sauce B

2 kiwifruit, peeled and pureed
2 tablespoons chicken broth
1 tablespoon lemon juice
2 teaspoons sugar
⅛ teaspoon salt

2 teaspoons cornstarch dissolved in 1 tablespoon water

◆Method

1. Combine marinade ingredients in a bowl. Cut beef into pieces about 3 inches wide and 6 inches long. Remove fillet from each chicken breast half; reserve for other uses. Split each breast half horizontally into three pieces. Lightly pound with a mallet to make pieces about the same size as the beef. Add the beef and chicken to the marinade and turn to coat. Let stand for 10 minutes.

2. Cut apple, kiwifruit, mango, and pear into thick matchstick pieces. Place 1 piece each of apple and kiwifruit on a short edge of each beef slice (stack 2 slices of beef together if they are too thin); roll up and secure with a wooden pick. Repeat procedure, filling and rolling each chicken slice with 1 piece each of mango and pear.

3. Heat oil in a wide frying pan over low heat. Add chicken rolls; cook, covered, for 2 minutes. Add beef rolls, cook, covered, for 3 minutes. Turn rolls occasionally so they brown lightly on all sides. Arrange chicken and beef rolls in a divided serving plate. Cover with foil to keep warm.

4. Combine Sauce A ingredients in a saucepan; bring to a boil over medium heat. Combine Sauce B ingredients in another saucepan; bring to a boil over medium heat. Add cornstarch solution and cook, stirring until sauce boils and thickens. Pour Sauce A over beef rolls, pour Sauce B over chicken rolls and serve.

Makes 4 to 6 servings

Stuffed Chicken Wings

◆**Ingredients**

3 dried black mushrooms

◆**Marinade**

1 tablespoon soy sauce
2 teaspoons cornstarch
¼ teaspoon salt
¼ teaspoon sugar

8 large chicken wings, middle sections only
2 tablespoons julienned cooked ham
¼ carrot, julienned
3 green onions, cut into 2 inch pieces
2 tablespoons butter

◆**Sauce**

3 tablespoons satay sauce
1 tablespoon soy sauce

1 teaspoon sesame oil
½ teaspoon sugar
¼ teaspoon white pepper

½ teaspoon cornstarch dissolved in 1 teaspoon water

◆**Method**

1. Soak mushrooms in warm water until softened, about 15 minutes; drain. Trim and discard stems. Thinly slice caps.

2. Combine marinade ingredients in a bowl. Using a heavy cleaver, chop both ends off each chicken wing middle section. Push out the two bones in each piece. Add chicken to marinade and stir to coat. Let stand for 10 minutes. Lift chicken from marinade; stuff a few pieces of mushroom, ham, carrot, and green onion in each wing.

3. Melt butter in a wide frying pan over medium heat. Add stuffed wings and cook until golden brown and tender, 2 to 3 minutes per side. Turn off heat and keep warm.

4. Combine sauce ingredients in a saucepan; bring to a boil over medium heat. Add cornstarch solution and cook, stirring, until sauce boils and thickens. Place wings on a serving plate and glaze each with a spoonful of sauce.

Makes 8 servings

TIPS

Blanching chicken wings tightens the skin and meat, which makes deboning a much easier job.

Drunken Squab

◆ Ingredients

2 squab

◆ Marinade

¼ cup rice wine or dry sherry
2 teaspoons sesame oil
1 teaspoon salt

◆ Cooking Liquid

2 cups water
1 tablespoon oyster-flavored sauce
2 teaspoons ginger juice
1 teaspoon dark soy sauce
1 teaspoon sesame oil
1 teaspoon sugar
¼ teaspoon salt
4 slices ginger, lightly crushed
3 green onions, cut into 2 inch
  pieces
1 tablespoon dried wolfberries
1 small piece ginseng (optional)

3 tablespoons cooking oil
½ cup Shao Hsing wine

◆ Method

1. Rinse squab and pat dry. Combine marinade ingredients in a bowl. Add squab and turn to coat. Refrigerate for 30 minutes.

2. Combine cooking liquid ingredients in a bowl.

3. Lift squab from marinade and pat dry with paper towels. Place a wok over medium-high heat until hot. Add oil, swirling to coat sides. Add squab and cook, turning, until browned on each side, 4 to 6 minutes total. Add cooking liquid. Bring to a boil; reduce heat, cover, and simmer until squab are tender, 10 to 12 minutes.

4. Remove squab from cooking liquid, let cool, then place in a plastic bag. Add Shao Hsing wine and seal bag. Refrigerate overnight, turning bag occasionally.

5. To serve, cut squab into bite-size pieces. Serve cold as an appetizer.

Note: Wolfberries are sold in Asian markets. If unavailable, substitute dried cranberries.

Culinary experts all over the world are most gracious in sharing their views on good food and culture.

TIPS

Dried fruits make great snacks and bring a pleasant texture contrast and tart-sweet flavor to braised dishes. But many Chinese dried fruits-wolfberries among them-also have reported medicinal benefits.

These small, bright red fruits of the medlar tree, have a wrinkled, chewy texture when dried and an intriguing flavor often compared to that of spiced apples. As if that weren't enough, they supposedly act as tonics for the kidneys and lungs. (Cranberries make tasty substitutes and have long been used to treat kidney infections, to boot.)

Makes 4 to 6 servings

Steamed Beef in Ti Leaves

◆ Ingredients

3 dried black mushrooms
½ cup chicken broth

◆ Marinade

¼ cup chicken broth
2 tablespoons soy sauce
1 tablespoon hoisin sauce
½ teaspoon cornstarch
¼ teaspoon ground toasted Sichuan peppercorns

½ pound tender boneless beef
¼ cup shredded bamboo shoots
6 fresh ti leaves, stems trimmed

◆ Method

1. Soak mushrooms in warm water until softened, about 15 minutes, drain. Trim and discard stems. Thinly slice caps. Bring chicken broth to a boil in a saucepan. Add mushrooms and cook for 2 minutes; drain.

2. Combine marinade ingredients in a bowl. Cut beef into thick matchstick pieces. Place beef, mushrooms, and bamboo shoots in marinade and stir to coat. Refrigerate for 30 minutes.

3. Place ti leaves, vein side up, on work surface. In center of each leaf, place about ¼ cup of meat mixture. Fold edges of each leaf over filling to make a closed packet. Place packets, folded side down, on a heat-proof serving dish.

4. Prepare a wok for steaming. Place dish in steamer; cover and steam over high heat for 8 to 10 minutes. Remove from steamer and serve.

Note: Ti leaves are widely available from florists. If you cannot find ti leaves, substitute parchment paper or aluminum foil.

Note: To toast Sichuan peppercorns, place them in a small frying pan over low heat; cook, shaking pan frequently, until they are aromatic. Immediately remove from pan to cool. Coarsely grind in a spice grinder. Use as needed; store remainder at room temperature in a tightly covered jar.

Since ancient times, bamboo has been a versatile material for countless household tools and kitchen utensils. And the young shoots from bamboo are absolutely delicious for so many dishes.

Makes 6 servings

Shrimp and Pork Balls

◆ Shrimp Balls

2 dried black mushrooms
½ pound medium raw shrimp
1 teaspoon cornstarch
¼ teaspoon salt

◆ Pork Balls

¼ pound ground pork
½ egg white, lightly beaten
1¼ teaspoons cornstarch
¼ teaspoon salt

◆ Sauce

¼ cup chicken broth
2 tablespoons oyster-flavored sauce
1 tablespoon soy sauce
2 teaspoons rice wine or dry sherry
2 teaspoons sesame oil
¼ teaspoon sugar
¼ teaspoon white pepper

2 tablespoons cooking oil
2 slices ginger, minced

1 jalapeño chile, seeded and thinly sliced
½ cup canned straw mushrooms, drained
1 teaspoon cornstarch dissolved in 2 teaspoons water

◆ Method

1. Prepare shrimp balls: Soak mushrooms in warm water until softened, about 15 minutes; drain. Trim and discard stems. Finely chop caps. Shell, devein, and finely chop shrimp. In a bowl, combine shrimp, mushrooms, cornstarch, and salt; mix to form a smooth paste. Roll mixture into 10 to 12 balls. Repeat process with pork ball ingredients, making 8 to 10 balls.

2. Bring a pot of water to a boil. Add shrimp and pork balls. Reduce heat to medium; cook for 3 minutes. Drain.

3. Combine sauce ingredients in a bowl.

4. Place a wok over high heat until hot. Add oil, swirling to coat sides. Add ginger and chile; cook, stirring, until fragrant, about 10 seconds. Add shrimp balls, pork balls, and straw mushrooms; stir-fry for 2 minutes. Add sauce; simmer over medium heat for 3 minutes. Add cornstarch solution and cook, stirring, until sauce boils and thickens. Transfer to a serving plate and serve.

Note: As a time saver, look for ready-made shrimp balls and pork balls in Asian markets.

Makes 4 to 6 servings

Two-flavored Beef

◆ **Ingredients**

½ pound russet potatoes, peeled and shredded
Cooking oil for deep-frying
¾ pound tender boneless beef

◆ **Marinade**

2 tablespoons soy sauce
2 teaspoons rice wine or dry sherry
2 teaspoons cornstarch
½ teaspoon sugar

◆ **Seasoning A**

¼ cup sweet and sour sauce
½ teaspoon chili garlic sauce

◆ **Seasoning B**

2 teaspoons water
1 teaspoon soy sauce
1 teaspoon curry powder
¼ teaspoon salt
¼ teaspoon sugar

2 tablespoons cooking oil
½ medium onion, cubed
1 apple, peeled and cubed
1 cup cubed mango
½ red bell pepper, seeded and cut into diamond-shape pieces

◆ **Method**

1. Rinse shredded potato in water; squeeze well to remove as much moisture as possible and pat dry with paper towels. Heat oil for deep-frying in a wok to 350°F. Spread half of potato over a 6 inch wire strainer. Nest a second strainer on top and immerse strainers in oil. Deep-fry until potatoes are golden brown, 3 to 4 minutes. Remove potato basket and drain on paper towels. Repeat with remaining potatoes. Place baskets on serving plates.

2. Cut beef into bite-size pieces. Place in a bowl with marinade ingredients and stir to coat. Let stand for 10 minutes. Combine seasoning A ingredients in a small bowl; combine seasoning B ingredients in a saucepan.

3. Place a wok over high heat until hot. Add the 2 tablespoons oil, swirling to coat sides. Add beef and onion; stir-fry for 1 minute. Add apple, mango, and bell pepper; stir-fry for 2 minutes.

4. Remove half of mixture and place in saucepan with seasoning B. Add seasoning A to wok and cook for 1 minute. Cook the meat in saucepan with seasoning B for 1 minute. Serve each portion in a potato basket.

Makes 4 to 6 servings

Beef Rolls with Satay Sauce

◆ Ingredients

8 dried black mushrooms

3 tablespoons shredded Sichuan preserved vegetable

⅔ cup chicken broth

¼ carrot, shredded

½ cup shredded celery

6 pieces tender boneless beef, sliced ¼ inch thick, cut into pieces 3 by 5 inches

◆ Marinade

1 tablespoon soy sauce

½ teaspoon cornstarch

½ teaspoon salt

½ teaspoon sugar

◆ Sauce

¼ cup chicken broth

2 teaspoons satay sauce

2 teaspoons soy sauce

1 teaspoon sesame paste

½ teaspoon sugar

2 tablespoons cooking oil

½ teaspoon cornstarch dissolved in 1 teaspoon water

◆ Method

1. Soak mushrooms in warm water until softened, about 15 minutes. Trim and discard stems. Thinly slice caps. Soak preserved vegetable in water for 10 minutes to reduce saltiness; drain. Bring chicken broth to a boil in a saucepan. Add mushrooms and simmer for 10 minutes; drain. Add carrot, celery, and preserved vegetable to mushrooms; mix lightly.

2. Pound beef lightly with a mallet. Combine marinade ingredients in a bowl. Add beef and stir to coat. Let stand for 10 minutes.

Combine sauce ingredients in a saucepan.

3. Make each roll: Place a rounded tablespoon of mushroom mixture across a narrow end of a beef slice; roll meat around filling and secure with a wooden pick.

4. Place a wide non-stick frying pan over medium heat until hot. Add oil, swirling to coat sides. Add beef rolls; cook until golden brown, 2 to 3 minutes on each side. Remove to a serving plate and keep warm.

5. Bring sauce to a boil over medium heat. Add cornstarch solution and cook, stirring, until sauce boils and thickens. Spoon sauce over beef rolls and serve.

TIPS

The spicy flavors of Sichuan province wouldn't be the same without sesame paste, a thick concoction made from toasted white sesame seeds. Sold in jars in stores, you can recognize it by its golden-brown to light, gray-brown color. Once you get it home, use it in anything that a roasted, nutty aroma and flavor would enhance-sauces, dips, dressing, and marinades all come to mind. You'll normally find a layer of oil on top of the paste when you first open a jar. Pour off this layer, scoop out the amount of paste you need, and, to prevent the paste from drying, pour on a fresh layer of oil-preferably sesame seed, but any mild-flavored vegetable oil will do-before storing the jar. And where should you store it? Keep opened jars of sesame paste in the refrigerator, where they'll keep for several months.

Makes 6 servings

Savory Beef Stew

◆ Ingredients

5 dried black mushrooms

2 dried bean curd sticks

◆ Braising Sauce

1½ cups chicken broth

1½ cups water

½ cup dry red wine

2 tablespoons hoisin sauce

1 teaspoon sugar

2 tablespoons cooking oil

1 pound boneless beef chuck

4 slices ginger, lightly crushed

4 cloves garlic, lightly crushed

1 pound daikon, roll cut

1 large carrot, roll cut

4 green onions, cut into 2 inch pieces

◆ Method

1. Soak mushrooms in warm water to cover until softened, about 15 minutes; drain. Trim and discard stems. Quarter caps. Soak bean curd sticks in warm water to cover until softened, about 15 minutes; drain and cut into 2 inch pieces.

2. Combine braising sauce ingredients in a bowl.

3. Heat oil in a 5-quart pan over medium-high heat. Add beef and brown lightly on all sides, 5 to 6 minutes. Add ginger and garlic; cook, stirring, until fragrant, about 10 seconds. Add braising sauce. Bring to a boil; reduce heat, cover, and simmer until meat is tender, about 1½ hours.

4. Add mushrooms, bean curd sticks, daikon, carrot, and green onions to pan. Cover and simmer until vegetables are tender when pierced, about 30 minutes.

Note: If bean curd sticks are not available, you can substitute extra-firm tofu or pressed tofu which is available in most health food stores or Asian grocery stores.

TIPS

The soybean is a culinary one-man band. It appears in China's favorite sauces and pastes (soy sauce is only one among many), it's indispensable in all types of bean curd, and soy milk wouldn't exist without it. Neither would the popular bean curd sticks found in this hearty beef stew. How does a soybean turn into a long, crinkled, buff-colored stick? In a roundabout way, to be sure: During bean curd production, a heated slurry of soybeans and water (which becomes soy milk itself) forms a skin on top in the same way that a pan of heated milk does. Skim off that skin, gently crinkle it, and lay it over a rail to dry, and you wind up with brittle bean curd sticks. Once soaked in warm water, they develop a chewy, meaty texture and bland flavor that "wears" the flavors of whatever rich sauce, stew, or gravy it's in like a tasty disguise. But bean curd sticks needn't disguise themselves; they can wear their soybean heritage with pride!

Makes 4 to 6 servings

Eight-flavored Pork Chops

◆ Marinade

2 stalks lemongrass, bottom 6 inches, minced

2 slices ginger, minced

2 tablespoons rice wine or dry sherry

1 tablespoon soy sauce

2 teaspoons cornstarch

4 pork chops, cut ½-inch thick

◆ Sauce

½ cup chicken broth

⅓ cup seasoned rice vinegar

¼ cup pineapple juice

3 tablespoons rice wine or dry sherry

2 teaspoons chili garlic sauce

1 teaspoon sugar

¼ teaspoon salt

3 tablespoons cooking oil

1 medium onion, diced

½ red bell pepper, seeded and diced

½ cup diced pineapple

1 tablespoon cornstarch dissolved in 2 tablespoons water

◆ Method

1. Combine marinade ingredients in a bowl. Add meat and turn to coat. Let stand for 20 minutes.

2. Combine sauce ingredients in a bowl.

3. Lift meat from marinade and pat dry with paper towels. Place a wok over medium heat until hot. Add 2 tablespoons of the oil, swirling to coat sides. Add meat and pan-fry until meat is golden brown and no longer pink in center, 4 to 5 minutes per side. Remove to a serving platter.

4. Heat remaining 1 tablespoon oil in wok over high heat. Add onion; stir-fry for 1 minute. Add bell pepper and pineapple; stir-fry for 1 minute. Add sauce; cook for another minute. Add cornstarch solution and cook, stirring, until sauce boils and thickens. Serve sauce alongside pork chops.

Makes 4 servings

Steamed Cabbage Pillows

◆ **Ingredients**

4 dried black mushrooms

2 tablespoons dried shrimp

◆ **Marinade**

2 tablespoons soy sauce

2 teaspoons rice wine or dry sherry

1 teaspoon cornstarch

¼ teaspoon white pepper

¼ pound medium raw shrimp, shelled, deveined, and finely chopped

¼ pound boneless, skinless chicken, finely chopped

1 tablespoon chopped cilantro

◆ **Sauce**

⅓ cup chicken broth

1 tablespoon oyster-flavored sauce

2 teaspoons rice wine or dry sherry

½ teaspoon sugar

4 - 6 large napa cabbage leaves

½ teaspoon cornstarch dissolved in 1 teaspoon water

◆ **Method**

1. In separate bowls, soak dried mushrooms and dried shrimp in warm water until cover until softened, about 15 minutes; drain. Discard mushroom stems and coarsely chop caps. Finely chop shrimp. Combine marinade ingredients in a bowl. Add raw shrimp, chicken, cilantro, mushrooms, and dried shrimp; mix well. Let stand for 10 minutes.

2. Combine sauce ingredients in a saucepan.

3. In a large pot of simmering water, parboil cabbage leaves just until limp, about 2 minutes. Drain, rinse with cold water, and drain again. Make each pillow: Place a leaf on work surface with stem end facing you. Spread ¼ cup of shrimp filling in center of leaf. Fold in top, bottom, and sides of leaf to form a square shape. Place pillows, folded side down, in a heat-proof dish.

4. Prepare a wok for steaming. Place dish in steamer. Cover and steam over high heat for 8 minutes. Remove from steamer and transfer pillows to a serving plate. Bring sauce ingredients to a boil over medium heat. Add cornstarch solution and cook, stirring, until sauce boils and thickens. Pour sauce over cabbage pillows and serve.

TIPS

Unlike grinding meat with a grinder, when chopping meat with a cleaver, pressure is unevenly applied to the muscle fibers of the meat. Subsequently, less proteins are lost because less cells are destroyed. Hand-chopped meats have a fresher taste and better texture than machine-ground meats.

Makes 4 to 6 servings

Pork with Spicy Garlic Sauce

◆ Ingredients

2 cups water

4 slices ginger, lightly crushed

2 green onions, cut into 2 inch pieces, lightly crushed

¾ pound boneless piece of pork leg or butt

◆ Sauce

¼ cup chicken broth

1 tablespoon chili garlic sauce

1 tablespoon soy sauce

1 teaspoon dark soy sauce

1 teaspoon rice vinegar

1 teaspoon rice wine or dry sherry

1 teaspoon sesame oil

½ teaspoon ground toasted Sichuan peppercorns (page 56)

½ teaspoon sugar

1 teaspoon sesame seeds

1 tablespoon cooking oil

4 cloves garlic, minced

½ teaspoon cornstarch dissolved in 1 teaspoon water

1 tablespoon chopped cilantro

◆ Method

1. Place water, ginger, and green onions in a 2-quart pan and bring to a boil. Place pork in pan; cover and simmer until meat is no longer pink in center when cut, 12 to 15 minutes. Remove meat from cooking liquid and let cool. Thinly slice meat and arrange on a serving plate.

2. Combine sauce ingredients in a bowl.

3. Place sesame seeds in a small frying pan over medium heat; cook, shaking pan frequently, until seeds are lightly browned, 3 to 4 minutes. Immediately remove from pan to cool.

4. Place a wok over high heat until hot. Add oil, swirling to coat sides. Add garlic and stir-fry until fragrant, about 10 seconds. Add sauce ingredients and bring to a boil. Add cornstarch solution and cook, stirring, until sauce boils and thickens. Pour sauce over sliced pork. Sprinkle with sesame seeds and cilantro.

Makes 4 to 6 servings

Lotus Root Cakes

◆ Marinade

1 tablespoon oyster-flavored sauce
2 teaspoons cornstarch
1 teaspoon sesame oil
¼ teaspoon salt
¼ teaspoon sugar
¼ teaspoon white pepper

¼ pound medium raw shrimp, shelled, deveined, and finely chopped
¼ pound ground pork
3 tablespoons chopped cilantro
1 green onion, minced
2 sections lotus root
Cornstarch for dusting
3 tablespoons cooking oil
¼ cup chicken broth
Ketchup

◆ Method

1. Combine marinade ingredients in a bowl. Add shrimp, pork, cilantro, and green onion; mix well. Let stand for 10 minutes.

2. Peel lotus root; cut into ½-inch thick slices. In a pot of boiling water, parboil lotus root for 2 minutes. Drain, rinse with cold water, and drain again; pat dry with paper towels. Make each cake: Spread 2 teaspoons shrimp mixture on a slice of lotus root. Smooth surface with a wet knife. Dust each side of lotus root cake with cornstarch; shake to remove excess.

3. Place a wide frying pan over medium heat until hot. Add oil, swirling to coat sides. Place cakes in pan, shrimp side down. Cook until lightly browned, about 1 minute. Add chicken broth; cover and cook for another 2 to 3 minutes. Turn lotus cakes over; cook, uncovered, 1 to 2 minutes or until browned.

4. Arrange lotus cakes on a serving platter. Serve with ketchup.

Note: If lotus root is unavailable, substitute potato, sweet potato, or any other starchy root vegetable.

TIPS

The tough parts that separate the sections of a lotus root are usually discarded. In China, however, they are reserved, sun-dried, and used in soups. Chinese herbalists believe that this part of the lotus root helps increase blood circulation.

Makes 4 to 6 servings

Tofu with Shrimp Paste

◆ Sauce

⅓ cup chicken broth
1 tablespoon soy sauce
2 teaspoons hoisin sauce
2 teaspoons chili garlic sauce
1 teaspoon sesame oil
1 teaspoon tomato paste
1 teaspoon sugar

¾ pound firm tofu
Cornstarch for dusting
4 tablespoons cooking oil
2 shallots, finely chopped
2 cloves garlic, minced
1 jalapeño chile, seeded and minced

1 teaspoon crumbled shrimp paste
½ teaspoon cornstarch dissolved in 1 teaspoon water

◆ Method

1. Combine sauce ingredients in a bowl.

2. Drain tofu; cut into 1½ inch by 1½ inch by ½ inch pieces. Dust tofu pieces with cornstarch; shake to remove excess.

3. Place a wok over high heat until hot. Add 2 tablespoons of the oil swirling to coat sides. Place tofu in pan; pan-fry until golden brown, 2 to 3 minutes on each side. Transfer tofu to a serving platter.

4. Return wok to high heat and heat the remaining 2 tablespoons oil. Add shallots, garlic, chile, and shrimp paste; stir-fry until fragrant, about 10 seconds. Add sauce and bring to a boil. Add cornstarch solution and cook, stirring, until sauce boils and thickens. Pour sauce over tofu and serve.

TIPS

Music may soothe the savage beast, but a little cooking turns pungent, slightly fishy-smelling shrimp paste into a mellow, mildly salty, and almost indispensable flavoring ingredient in stir-fries, rice dishes, and savory braised casseroles. Made from salted fermented shrimp, the pinkish-gray sauce has an odor that reminds me of childhood fishing trips. The flavor gets my mind wandering too-wandering right into the kitchen to stir up a little something with some shrimp paste.

Makes 4 to 6 servings

Winter Melon Pockets

◆ Ingredients

10 dried black mushrooms

10 dried cloud ears

1 pound winter melon

1 ounce thinly sliced cooked ham, cut to fit winter melon pockets

◆ Sauce

2 tablespoons cooking oil

3 tablespoons chopped button mushrooms

3 tablespoons chopped fresh shiitake mushrooms (stems removed)

2 tablespoons chopped cooked ham

1 cup chicken broth

1 tablespoon vegetarian oyster-flavored sauce

1 teaspoon rice wine or dry sherry

½ teaspoon chili garlic sauce

½ teaspoon sesame oil

⅛ teaspoon sugar

2 teaspoons cornstarch dissolved in 1 tablespoon water

◆ Method

1. In separate bowls, soak dried mushrooms and cloud ears in warm water to cover until softened, about 15 minutes; drain. Discard mushroom stems and halve caps. Coarsely chop cloud ears.

2. Trim hard skin off winter melon; cut flesh crosswise into ½ inch thick slices. In a pot of boiling water, parboil melon just until slightly softened, 2 to 3 minutes. Drain, rinse with cold water, and drain again. Make each pocket: Cut a piece of melon horizontally almost all the way through; open it up like a book. Place half a black mushroom and a slice of ham inside the melon; close the pocket. Place melon pockets on a heat-proof dish.

3. Prepare a wok for steaming. Place dish in steamer. Cover and steam over high heat for 5 minutes. Remove from steamer and transfer winter melon to a serving plate. Keep warm.

4. Prepare sauce: Place a wok over high heat until hot. Add oil, swirling to coat sides. Add button and shiitake mushrooms, cloud ears, and ham; stir-fry for 1 minute. Add remaining sauce ingredients; bring to a boil and cook for 3 minutes. Add cornstarch solution and cook, stirring, until sauce boils and thickens. Pour sauce over winter melon and serve.

TIPS

There is a vegetarian condiment known as "mushroom leg" which is made with dried black mushroom stems. The stems are soaked, trimmed, air-dried, and deep-fried. They are then stir-fried with rice wine and a touch of red chiles until fragrant. The cooked stems make a great condiment for rice and noodles.

Makes 4 to 6 servings

Vegetables in Pumpkin Bowl

◆ Ingredients

2 tablespoons dried lily buds (optional)

1 small pumpkin, such as kabocha, 1½ to 2 pounds

◆ Seasonings

¼ cup chicken broth or water

2 tablespoons vegetarian oyster-flavored sauce

1 teaspoon rice wine or dry sherry

1 teaspoon sesame oil

2 tablespoons cooking oil

1 slice ginger, minced

2 cloves garlic, minced

⅓ cup sliced celery

⅓ cup canned straw mushrooms

6 water chestnuts, sliced

¼ carrot, thinly sliced

2 tablespoons canned lotus seeds (optional)

½ teaspoon cornstarch dissolved in 1 teaspoon water

◆ Method

1. Soak lily buds in warm water until softened, about 15 minutes; drain. Discard hard tips from lily buds.

2. Prepare pumpkin bowl: Remove a thin slice from bottom of pumpkin so it stands upright. Cut off top one-fourth of pumpkin; discard seeds. With a small knife, remove a thin layer of flesh without tearing shell; slice flesh to make about ¼ cup. Prepare a wok for steaming. Place pumpkin in steamer; cover and steam over high heat until pumpkin flesh is tender, 8 to 10 minutes. Remove pumpkin from steamer.

3. Combine seasoning ingredients in a bowl.

4. Place a wok over high heat until hot. Add oil, swirling to coat sides. Add ginger and garlic and cook, stirring, until fragrant, about 10 seconds. Add sliced pumpkin flesh, celery, straw mushrooms, water chestnuts, carrot, lotus seeds, lily buds, and seasonings. Reduce heat to low; cover and cook until vegetables are crisp-tender, 4 to 5 minutes. Add cornstarch solution and cook, stirring, until sauce boils and thickens. Spoon vegetable mixture into pumpkin bowl and serve.

This melon may be the perfect size for hurtling down the 50-yard line, but I'd rather carry it gently into my kitchen where I can turn it into a delicious dish.

TIPS

The fashion for decorating salads with edible flowers may seem more style than substance. But the appearance of lily buds in all sorts of Chinese dishes-from Hot and Sour soup, to Mu Shu, to this vegetable assortment served in a pumpkin bowl-serves a genuine purpose. Usually dried, the short brown strands are delicately musky and a little bit sweet as well. And according to specialists of Chinese herbal medicine, they act as tonics and sedatives.

Makes 4 to 6 servings

Asparagus and Potato Croquettes

◆ Ingredients

1   pound russet potatoes, peeled and quartered
¼ cup chopped Sichuan preserved vegetable
1   tablespoon chopped cilantro
5   large asparagus spears

◆ Dough

½ cup wheat starch
½ teaspoon salt
½ teaspoon sugar
½ cup boiling water

Cooking oil for deep-frying
2 eggs, lightly beaten
2 cups panko (Japanese bread crumbs)
Pepper salt
Sweet and sour sauce

◆ Method

1. In a pot of water, boil potatoes until soft, about 15 minutes; drain and mash. Soak preserved vegetable in water for 10 minutes to reduce saltiness; drain. Combine mashed potatoes, preserved vegetable, and cilantro.

2. Trim asparagus; cut into 16 pieces, each about 2½ inches long. In a pot of boiling water, cook asparagus until barely tender, 1 to 2 minutes. Drain, rinse with cold water, and drain again.

3. Prepare dough: Combine wheat starch, salt, and sugar in a bowl. Add boiling water, stirring until dough hold together. Add mashed potato mixture and mix well. Roll dough into a cylinder about 8 inches long; cut dough into 16 equal portions. Shape each croquette: Flatten a portion of dough, place one piece of asparagus in the middle, and roll dough into a cylindrical shape, enclosing asparagus.

4. In a wok, heat oil for deep-frying to 350°F. Dip each croquette in egg, then coat with panko. Deep-fry croquettes, a few at a time, until golden brown, 4 to 5 minutes. Remove and drain on paper towels. Arrange croquettes on a serving plate. Serve with pepper salt or sweet and sour sauce.

Makes 4 to 6 servings

Skewered Vegetables

◆ Marinade

2 tablespoons Chinese barbecue
   sauce
2 tablespoons soy sauce

6 fresh kumquats
6 button mushrooms, stems
   trimmed
6 fresh shiitake mushrooms, stems
   trimmed
6 canned straw mushrooms
6 water chestnuts
½ green bell pepper, seeded and cut
   into diamond-shape pieces
½ red bell pepper, seeded and cut
   into diamond-shape pieces

◆ Sauce

¼ cup chicken broth or water
1 tablespoon Chinese barbecue
   sauce
1 tablespoon vegetarian oyster-
   flavored sauce
1 tablespoon rice wine or dry
   sherry
1 teaspoon honey

6 wooden skewers
1 tablespoon cooking oil
1 teaspoon cornstarch dissolved in
   2 teaspoons water

◆ Method

1. Combine marinade ingredients
   in a bowl. Add kumquats, all
   mushrooms, water chestnuts,
   and bell peppers; stir to coat. Let
   stand for 10 minutes.

2. Combine sauce ingredients in a
   saucepan.

3. Prepare skewers: Thread one
   kumquat and one of each
   vegetable on a skewer. Place a
   grill pan over medium heat until
   hot. Brush with 1 teaspoon of
   the oil. Place skewers on grill pan
   and cook, turning as needed and
   brushing with the remaining 2
   teaspoons oil, until vegetables are
   crisp-tender. Remove to a
   serving plate.

4. Bring sauce ingredients to a boil
   over medium heat. Add
   cornstarch solution and cook,
   stirring, until sauce boils and
   thickens. Pour sauce over
   skewers and serve.

Makes 4 to 6 servings

TIPS

From autumn through spring, search your produce market for small, oval fruits that look almost like doll-sized oranges. Actually, these aren't oranges at all. Rather, they're kumquats, the perfect citrus fruits for people who don't like to peel citrus fruits. Why? Because the whole package is edible, from the sweet-tart pulp to the mildly sweet peel, which ranges in color from bright orange to golden yellow. Enjoy kumquats as snacks on their own, popping them in your mouth as if they were grapes. They also make great additions to fruit salads. Skewered with mushrooms and other vegetables, they liven up this recipe for Grilled Rainbow Vegetables with their golden color and tangy flavor.

Asparagus Seaweed Bundles

◆ Ingredients

1 dried bean curd sheet

2 tablespoons shredded preserved vegetable

1 cup chicken broth or water

8 large asparagus tips, each 4 inches long

¼ carrot, shredded

¼ red bell pepper, julienned

◆ Sauce

½ cup chicken broth or water

1 tablespoon vegetarian oyster-flavored sauce

1 tablespoon finely diced green bell pepper

1 tablespoon finely diced red bell pepper

1 teaspoon sugar

½ teaspoon soy sauce

Flour paste for sealing

2 teaspoons cooking oil

1 sheet Japanese seaweed (nori), cut into eight 1 inch strips

◆ Method

1. Soak dried bean curd sheet in warm water to cover until softened, about 15 minutes; drain and cut into eight 3 by 4 inch pieces. Soak preserved vegetable in water 10 minutes to reduce saltiness; drain.

2. Bring chicken broth to a boil in a saucepan. Add asparagus and cook for 2 minutes. Lift out asparagus and set aside. Add carrot, bell pepper, and preserved vegetable to broth; cook for 30 seconds; drain. Combine sauce ingredients in a saucepan.

3. Make each bundle: Spoon a rounded teaspoon of carrot mixture on the long end of a piece of bean curd sheet. Fold edge over and roll, forming a tight roll. Seal edges with flour paste. Place a wide frying pan over medium heat until hot. Add oil, swirling to coat sides. Place bundles in pan and cook until golden brown, 2 minutes on each side. Remove from pan. Place one asparagus tip on each bundle. Wrap a strip of seaweed around the middle of each bundle; brush edges with water and press to seal. Arrange bundles on a serving plate.

4. Bring sauce ingredients to a boil over medium heat. Add cornstarch solution and cook, stirring, until sauce boils and thickens. Serve sauce alongside asparagus bundles.

TIPS

Bean curd sheets, the dried skins that form atop heated vats of soymilk, really help Chinese cooks keep everything "wrapped up." After soaking in warm water to soften, the sheets become pliable enough to wrap, egg roll-style, around meat and vegetable fillings. Alternatively, crumble dried sheets into stews and savory soups and braised dishes-they soften to a chewy texture and develop a flavor that's both meaty and accented with whatever rich sauces and liquids they cook in.

Makes 4 to 6 servings

Seafood Chowder

◆ Ingredients

6 dried black mushrooms

◆ Marinade

1 egg white
1 tablespoon rice wine or dry sherry
1 tablespoon cornstarch

¼ pound firm white fish fillet, cut into ½-inch cubes
¼ pound medium raw shrimp, shelled, deveined, and diced
¼ pound sea scallops, diced
6 cups chicken broth
2 tablespoons cooking oil
2 tablespoons butter
2 teaspoons shredded ginger
1 green onion, shredded
⅓ cup sliced bamboo shoots
¼ cup frozen peas, thawed
¼ cup Shao Hsing wine
¼ teaspoon white pepper
¼ cup cornstarch dissolved in ¼ cup water
2 egg whites, lightly beaten

◆ Method

1. Soak mushrooms in warm water to cover until softened, about 15 minutes; drain. Trim and discard stems. Dice caps.

2. Combine marinade ingredients in a bowl. Add fish, shrimp, and scallops and stir to coat. Let stand for 10 minutes.

3. Place broth in a pot and bring to a boil; reduce heat so broth simmers.

4. Heat a wide frying pan over high heat until hot. Add oil and butter. Add ginger and green onion and cook, stirring, until fragrant, about 10 seconds. Add seafood and stir-fry for 1 minute. Add mushrooms, bamboo shoots, and peas; stir-fry for 1 minute. Add wine and white pepper; mix well. Pour seafood mixture into broth and return to a simmer. Add cornstarch solution and cook, stirring, until soup boils and thickens. Turn off heat. Add egg whites, stirring until they form long threads. Serve in individual soup bowls.

Makes 4 to 6 servings

Meat Balls in Savory Broth

◆ Ingredients

6 dried black mushrooms

◆ Pork Balls

¼ pound ground pork
1 teaspoon chopped cilantro
1 tablespoon water
½ teaspoon cornstarch
½ teaspoon rice wine or dry sherry

◆ Beef Balls

¼ pound ground beef
1 teaspoon minced green onion
1 tablespoon water
1 teaspoon soy sauce
1 teaspoon cornstarch
½ teaspoon rice wine or dry sherry

◆ Fish Balls

¼ pound boneless white fish, minced

2 teaspoons cornstarch
½ teaspoon salt
¼ teaspoon white pepper

3 cups chicken broth
2 cups water
2 tablespoons chopped celery
1 jalapeño or serrano chile, seeded and sliced
2 tablespoons soy sauce
1 teaspoon sesame oil

◆ Method

1. Soak mushrooms in warm water to cover until softened, about 15 minutes; drain. Trim and discard stems. Thinly slice caps.

2. Combine pork ball ingredients in a bowl. Let stand for 10 minutes. Repeat with beef ball ingredients and fish ball ingredients. Separately, roll each mixture to make 1-inch balls.

3. Place broth and water in a pot and bring to a boil; reduce heat to medium. Add mushrooms, pork balls, and beef balls; cook for 2 minutes. Add fish balls, celery, chile, soy sauce, and sesame oil; cook for 3 to 4 minutes. Ladle soup into individual bowls and serve.

Note: Purchase ready-made pork, beef, and fish balls if they're available.

Makes 4 to 6 servings

Seafood and Pickled Vegetable Soup

◆ **Ingredients**

4 dried black mushrooms

1 tablespoon dried lily buds (optional)

⅓ cup julienned Sichuan preserved vegetable

◆ **Marinade**

2 tablespoons oyster-flavored sauce

2 tablespoons rice wine or dry sherry

½ teaspoon salt

½ teaspoon white pepper

¼ pound firm white fish fillet, sliced

¼ pound medium raw shrimp, shelled, deveined, and diced

¼ pound sea scallops, diced

◆ **Seasonings**

1 tablespoon oyster-flavored sauce

2 teaspoons sugar

1 teaspoon dark soy sauce

1 teaspoon sesame oil

3 cups chicken broth

2 tablespoons cooking oil

3 cloves garlic, sliced

⅔ cup sliced button mushrooms

1 small tomato, diced

1 tablespoon cornstarch dissolved in 2 tablespoons water

2 green onions, shredded

1 tablespoon chopped cilantro

◆ **Method**

1. In separate bowls, soak mushrooms and lily buds in warm water to cover until softened, about 15 minutes; drain. Trim and discard mushroom stems. Slice caps. Discard hard tips from lily buds. Soak preserved vegetable in water for 10 minutes to reduce saltiness; drain.

2. Combine marinade ingredients in a bowl. Add fish, shrimp, and scallops and stir to coat. Let stand for 10 minutes. Combine seasoning ingredients in a bowl.

3. Place broth in a pot and bring to a boil; reduce heat so broth simmers.

4. Place a wok over high heat until hot. Add oil, swirling to coat sides. Add garlic and cook, stirring, until lightly browned, 30 to 40 seconds. Add seafood, black mushrooms, and lily buds; stir-fry for 1 minute. Pour seafood mixture into broth. Add button mushrooms, preserved vegetable, and tomato. Return to a simmer and cook for 2 to 3 minutes. Add seasoning ingredients and cornstarch solution and cook, stirring, until soup boils and thickens. Add green onions and cilantro and serve.

Makes 4 to 6 servings

Curried Seafood over Rice

◆ Marinade

1 tablespoon rice wine or dry sherry

½ teaspoon cornstarch

¼ teaspoon salt

¼ cup diced (shelled and deveined) raw shrimp

¼ cup diced sea scallops

¼ cup diced cleaned squid

◆ Seasonings

1½ cups chicken broth

2 tablespoons unsweetened coconut milk

1 tablespoon curry powder

2 teaspoons soy sauce

½ teaspoon white pepper

2 tablespoons cooking oil

1 egg, lightly beaten

4 to 5 cups cooked long-grain rice

1 slice ginger, minced

¼ onion, diced

¼ carrot, diced

⅓ cup frozen peas, thawed

2 tablespoons butter

2 tablespoons all-purpose flour

◆ Method

1. Combine marinade ingredients in a bowl. Add shrimp, scallops, and squid and stir to coat. Let stand for 10 minutes. Combine seasoning ingredients in a bowl.

2. Place a wok over medium-high heat until hot. Add 1 tablespoon of the oil, swirling to coat sides. Add egg and cook until it is softly set; cut into small pieces with a spatula. Add rice and stir-fry for 2 minutes. Remove to a serving plate.

3. Return wok to medium heat. Add the remaining 1 tablespoon oil. Add ginger and onion and stir-fry until fragrant, about 10 seconds. Add seafood; stir-fry for 2 minutes. Add carrot and peas; stir-fry for 1 minute. Remove wok from heat.

4. Melt butter in a saucepan over medium heat. Add flour; cook, stirring, for 1 minute. Remove pan from heat and, using a wire whisk, gradually blend in seasoning ingredients. Return pan to heat and cook, stirring, until sauce comes to a boil. Add seafood mixture and mix well. Spoon sauce over rice and serve.

Makes 4 to 6 servings

Rice Noodle Soup

◆ Ingredients

½ pound fresh rice noodles

◆ Seasonings

2 tablespoons vegetarian oyster-flavored sauce

1 tablespoon soy sauce

¼ teaspoon sugar

2 tablespoons chopped Sichuan preserved vegetable

2 cups chicken broth

2 tablespoons cooking oil

1 jalapeno chile, seeded and julienned

¼ green bell pepper, seeded and julienned

¼ red bell pepper, seeded and julienned

⅓ cup julienned cooked ham

⅓ cup julienned celery

½ cup bean sprouts

◆ Method

1. In a large pot of boiling water, blanch rice noodles for 15 seconds; drain, rinse with cold water, and drain again. Place in a serving bowl. Combine seasoning ingredients in a bowl. Rinse preserved vegetable to reduce saltiness.

2. Place broth in a pot and bring to a boil; reduce heat so broth simmers.

3. Place a wok over high heat until hot. Add oil, swirling to coat sides. Add chile and stir-fry until fragrant, about 10 seconds. Add bell peppers and ham; stir-fry for 1 minute. Add celery, preserved vegetable, bean sprouts, and seasoning ingredients; stir-fry for 30 seconds. Pour over noodles. Ladle hot broth over noodles and serve.

Makes 4 to 6 servings

Pan-fried Noodles

◆ Ingredients

5 dried black mushrooms

¼ pound boneless, skinless chicken

◆ Marinade

1 teaspoon soy sauce

1 teaspoon cornstarch

¼ teaspoon white pepper

◆ Seasonings

1 cup chicken broth

2 tablespoons oyster-flavored sauce

1 tablespoon dark soy sauce

2 teaspoons soy sauce

2 teaspoons sesame oil

½ pound fresh thin egg noodles

5 tablespoons cooking oil

2 cloves garlic, minced

1 slice ginger, minced

1 rib celery, finely chopped

¼ red bell pepper, seeded and finely chopped

2 teaspoons cornstarch dissolved in 1 tablespoon water

◆ Method

1. Soak mushrooms in warm water to cover until softened, about 15 minutes; drain. Trim and discard mushroom stems. Thinly slice caps. Julienne chicken. Place in a bowl with marinade ingredients and stir to coat. Let stand for 10 minutes. Combine seasoning ingredients in a bowl.

2. In a large pot of boiling water, cook noodles for 30 seconds. Drain, rinse with cold water, and drain again. Place a wide frying pan over medium heat until hot. Add 3 tablespoons of the oil, swirling to coat sides. Spread noodles in pan. Cook, turning once, until golden brown and crispy, 3 to 4 minutes per side. Turn off heat.

3. Place a wok over high heat until hot. Add the remaining 2 tablespoons oil, swirling to coat sides. Add garlic and ginger and cook, stirring, until fragrant, about 10 seconds. Add chicken, mushrooms, celery, and bell pepper; stir-fry for 2 minutes. Add seasoning ingredients and bring to a boil. Add cornstarch solution and cook, stirring, until sauce boils and thickens.

4. Place noodle pancake on a serving plate and pour sauce over the top.

I was born in Guangzhou, where rice is a steady daily staple. However this doesn't mean that I don't enjoy "using my noodle" whenever I have a chance.

Makes 4 to 6 servings

Fruit Napoleon

◆ Ingredients

Cooking oil for deep-frying

16 wonton wrappers

◆ Sauce

½ cup water

⅓ cup sugar

¼ cup lemon juice

2 tablespoons orange-flavored liqueur

2 tablespoons cornstarch dissolved in 2 tablespoons water

1 cup fresh or canned lychees, halved and pitted

4 kiwifruit, peeled and sliced

1 cup strawberries, sliced

2 plums, halved, pitted, and sliced

½ cup canned mandarin oranges, drained

1 cup whipping cream

¼ cup powdered sugar

½ teaspoon vanilla extract

Mint sprigs for garnish

◆ Method

1. In a wok, heat oil for deep-frying to 350°F. Deep-fry wonton wrappers, a few at a time, until lightly browned, 15 to 20 seconds on each side. Remove and drain on paper towels.

2. Prepare sauce: Combine water, sugar, lemon juice, and liqueur in a small pan. Cook over medium heat, stirring frequently, until sugar dissolves. Add cornstarch solution and cook, stirring, until sauce boils and thickens. Let cool.

3. In a bowl, combine lychees, kiwifruit, strawberries, plums, and mandarin oranges. In another bowl, whip cream until frothy. Add powdered sugar and vanilla extract; whip until soft peaks form.

4. For each serving, place a wrapper on a dessert plate, top with a spoonful of cream and a spoonful of fruit. Repeat to make 3 or 4 layers. Drizzle sauce on top and garnish with mint.

Makes 4 to 6 servings

◆Ingredients

1 tablespoon black sesame seeds

2 teaspoons white sesame seeds

3 medium-firm, ripe bananas

¼ cup evaporated milk

1 tablespoon sugar

¼ cup dried apricots, chopped

¼ cup golden raisins

2 tablespoons packed brown sugar

1 tablespoon finely shredded orange peel

⅛ teaspoon cinnamon

1 tablespoon butter

◆Method

1. Place black sesame seeds in a small frying pan over medium heat; cook, shaking pan frequently, until seeds smell toasted, 3 to 4 minutes. Immediate remove from pan to cool. Repeat with white sesame seeds but cook until lightly browned, 3 to 4 minutes.

2. Preheat oven to 325°F.

3. Peel bananas. Cut 1 banana in chunks and place in blender with evaporated milk and sugar; blend until smooth. Halve the remaining 2 bananas lengthwise; arrange, cut side up, in a shallow baking dish. Sprinkle apricots, raisins, brown sugar, orange peel, and cinnamon over the top; dot with butter. Bake until bananas are heated through, 12 to 15 minutes.

4. Pour pureed banana mixture in a rimmed serving plate. Arrange baked bananas and dried fruits on top. Sprinkle with black and white sesame seeds. Serve hot.

Buttery Baked Bananas

Makes 4 to 6 servings

Mango Pudding

◆ Ingredients

2 mangoes, each about ¾ pound

1 ¼ cups cold water

2 envelopes unflavored gelatin

½ cup milk

⅔ cup sugar

½ cup unsweetened coconut milk

◆ Method

1. Peel mangoes and cut flesh from pits. Cut enough flesh into small cubes to make ¼ cup. Chop remaining flesh to make 1½ cups. Place chopped fruit in a blender with 1 cup of the cold water; puree until smooth.

2. In a bowl, sprinkle gelatin over the remaining ¼ cup cold water; let soften for 5 minutes.

3. Combine milk and sugar in a 2-quart pan. Cook, stirring, over medium-low heat until sugar dissolves; remove from heat. Add softened gelatin and stir until gelatin dissolves. Add coconut milk (shake can before opening to mix the heavy coconut cream with the thin coconut milk) and mango puree; whisk until blended. Fold in diced mango. Pour into 4 to 6 1-cup custard cups. Refrigerate until firm, 3 to 4 hours.

Makes 4 to 6 servings

Coconut Pudding

◆ Ingredients

1½ tablespoons unflavored gelatin
⅓ cup cold water
¾ cup boiling water
⅓ cup sugar
⅓ cup unsweetened coconut milk
3 egg whites
2 tablespoons shredded coconut

◆ Method

1. In a medium bowl, sprinkle gelatin over the cold water; let soften for 5 minutes. Add boiling water; stir until gelatin dissolves. Add sugar; stir until sugar dissolves. Stir in coconut milk (shake can before opening to mix the heavy coconut cream with the thin coconut milk). Refrigerate until mixture mounds slightly when dropped from a spoon.

2. With an electric mixer, beat egg whites until stiff peaks form. Using the same beaters, whip gelatin mixture until smooth. Fold egg whites into gelatin mixture. Pour into an 8 inch square pan. Refrigerate until firm, 3 to 4 hours.

3. Spread coconut in a pie pan; toast in a 350°F. oven, stirring frequently, until lightly browned, 4 to 5 minutes.

4. To serve, cut pudding into diamond-shaped pieces and garnish with coconut.

Makes 4 to 6 servings

Lemony Tofu Mousse

◆ Ingredients

2 slices white sandwich bread

1 package (16 ounces) soft tofu, drained

½ cup milk

3 eggs

⅔ cup sugar

2 teaspoons grated lemon peel

◆ Method

1. Trim bread crusts. Cut bread into ½ inch cubes.

2. Mash tofu. Place in a clean towel and squeeze to remove excess liquid. In a food processor, whirl tofu until smooth. Add bread, milk, eggs, and sugar; process until smooth. Stir in lemon peel. Pour tofu mixture into 4 to 6 1-cup custard cups.

3. Prepare a wok for steaming. Place custard cups in steamer; set a piece of wax paper loosely over cups. Cover and steam over medium heat until a knife inserted in center comes out clean, about 15 minutes.

4. Remove custard cups from steamer, let cool, then refrigerate until cold. Serve chilled.

Makes 4 to 6 servings

Black mushrooms, dried: open-capped mushrooms with brownish-black caps and tan gills; firm and chewy in texture, with meaty flavor that intensifies when dried; use sliced in stir-fries or chopped in dumpling fillings

Cellophane noodles: dried noodles made from mung bean starch (also called bean thread noodles); before using, soak in warm water until softened

Chile garlic paste: similar to brown bean paste but with dried chiles and often garlic, fermented black beans, and spices added for hot, nutty character; use in sauces and stir-fries for flavorful bite

Chinese five-spice powder: cocoa-colored powder made from cinnamon, cloves, fennel, Sichuan peppercorns, and star anise; adds sweet and spicy flavor to marinades, sauces, braised, and red-cooked dishes

Chinese rice wine: amber-colored liquid made from fermented glutinous rice and millet; aged 10 to 100 years; Shao Hsing, in eastern China, known for its high-quality rice wines; common ingredient in sauces and marinades

Cloud ears; dried: variety of dried black fungus with dark, leathery appearance; chewy and meaty in texture and bland in flavor when soaked to soften in warm water

Daikon: long, slender Japanese radish with crisp, white flesh and peppery taste; peeled and shredded for use as sushi garnish in Japan; enjoyed in stews and braised dishes in China; substitute potato or turnip if daikon is unavailable

Dark soy sauce: regular soy sauce with molasses added for darker color, thicker consistency, and slight sweetness; gives mahogany color and rich flavor to dips, sauces, stir-fries, and red-cooked dishes

Dried seaweed: deep-green sheets of washed, dried, and seasoned seaweed; used as wraps for sushi or shredded as garnish in soups and salads; called nori in Japan

Dried shrimp: small, dried, brine-preserved shrimp; chewy, highly flavored ingredients in soups and dumpling fillings; make tasty snacks on their own

Enoki mushrooms: pale-ivory, long-stemmed fresh mushrooms with tiny caps and delicate flavor; use in soups or salads, or as garnish

Fermented soybean paste: intensely flavored, thick mixture of whole ground fermented soybeans; available in cans or jars and used in bean curd and braised meat dishes

Longans: oval fruit with smooth brown shell; taste similar to lychees but are slightly smaller; available in cans and occasionally fresh; excellent in fruit salads or as snack

Lotus root: long, off-white, segmented roots used in soups and braised dishes for fibrous crunch; when sliced crosswise, reveals attractive, lacy holes that run length of root; substitute potato or other starchy vegetable if lotus root is unavailable

Lotus seeds: delicately flavored seeds available fresh, canned, or dried; often ground, sweetened, and used as paste in desserts; also used whole in stews and stir-fries

Lychees: small, round sweet fruit with juicy, pearly white flesh; fresh fruit has bumpy reddish-pink skin; usually available canned in syrup

Panko: toasted, Japanese-style breadcrumbs used in deep-frying;

coarser, larger, and crispier than Western-style breadcrumbs

Pickled ginger : brine-cured slices of fresh ginger soaked in solution of sugar and vinegar; occasionally dyed red; common condiment with sushi or garnish

Pressed bean curd: firm, compact bean curd with most of whey drained off; sold in flat cakes and bricks; often marinated with seasonings such as Chinese five-spice powder (marinated kinds have dark color); use in stews, salads, stir-fries, and vegetarian dishes

Satay sauce: classic Indonesian peanut sauce; often contains chiles, garlic, ginger, dark soy sauce, sesame oil, and shallots, among other ingredients

Shiitake mushrooms: similar to black mushrooms in color, texture and flavor; available fresh as well as dried; use in same manner as dried black mushrooms

Sichuan peppercorns: dried reddish-brown berries with warm, woodsy aroma and flavor; normally toasted to bring out their flavor and ground for use in sauces, stews, marinades, and red-cooked dishes

Sichuan preserved vegetables: dark-green and spicy-salty kohlrabi, mustard greens, napa cabbage, or turnips, preserved with chile powder and Sichuan peppercorns; finely chop for dumpling fillings or coarsely chop for soups and stews

Star anise: small, inedible, star-shaped pod with shiny reddish seed in each of eight points; adds distinct licorice flavor to stews, sauces, and braised dishes, removed after cooking

Tangerine peel, dried: wrinkled, dark-orange dried peel used to flavor soups, stews, and sauces; soak to soften and scrape off bitter white layer under peel before using

Tofu puffs: deep-fried tofu pieces with lightly crispy, golden-brown outside and spongy center; add to soups and stews, or scoop out center and stuff with fillings